MOM AND ME

An Informative Memoir of
Parental Caregiving

Photography by: Ms. Camille Mann of Photos by Camille
camillemann26@yahoo.com
Formatting by: Mr. Ryan Jenkins of Poetic Souls Inc./rd.jenkins@cox.net
Cover Designed by: Mr. Alex Holt of Heavens Gateway Media
/heavensgatewaymedia@gmail.com

ISBN 10: **0692246878**
ISBN 13: **978-0-692-24687-0**
LCCN Imprint Name: Dorcas Publishing, Newport News. Virginia

Dedication

This book was inspired by and is written in loving memory of my beloved parents, John and Dorothy Weathersby. I miss them both dearly. I thank God for giving me great parents who made every sacrifice to give me and my siblings a good home with two loving parents.

Acknowledgments

I would like to acknowledge and give thanks to God first and foremost. My relationship with God has allowed me to escape, survived, and recover from this twelve-year journey of care giving. I thank God for the many times prayers were answered.

The other mainstays in my life are my children. Carol M. Mann, Carley A. Mann, Corrine V. Mann, Clarisa D. Mann, Camille L. Mann, and Raquel A. Edmonds, who assisted me with hand-on care of my mother, their grandmother, and who made great sacrifices to be present and to stand with me in times of extreme difficulty. I love them with all of my heart, and I thank God for blessing me to have them in my life. Special thanks to my grandson, Javone Ransdell, who would stop playing with friends to come in and feed his great-grandmother or read to her. Also to my granddaughter, Aubrey Marie Sanchious, who gave her great-grandmother so much joy, especially having been born on her birthday. Being able to hold her meant the world to my mother, who passed away a year after her birth. I would also like to give special thanks to my two close friends, Prophetess Joan Bynum, of PJB Ministries International, and Apostle Demontae Edmonds, who held me up in prayer and supported me with words of encouragement and love throughout my journey. Thank you both for being such a blessing to me. Special thanks and acknowledgment to Pastors Lawrence and Dorothy Govan of Progressive Life Worship and Training Center, and to the entire Progressive Life family, for showing my mother so much love while she was alive and after her departure. If by chance I missed anyone, charge it to my head and not my heart.

Table of Contents

Table of Contents

Chapter 1

In the Beginning

My mom, Dorothy Weathersby, was born Dorothy Wright on January 24, 1932, in Harlem, New York. Her parents, my grandparents, were her father, Cliffon Wright, an immigrant who hailed from the beautiful British Virgin Islands of Barbados, and her mother, Maggie Martin, a domestic worker who struggled with alcoholism. My grandmother was born and raised on the Gullah Islands of South Carolina, as told to my mother by Aunt Lu. My mother saw Aunt Lu as a great woman of faith, who stopped the residence in their tracks upon hearing her fervent prayers to the Father each morning.

The earliest recollection Mom had was of my grandmother lying in the bed, unable to care for herself. She had been ill for some time and apparently felt her end was near. One day after Mom returned home from elementary school, her mother called her into the bedroom. Her mother beckoned her to come closer to the bed, where she had been lying for some weeks. Her mother instructed her to tell the social worker that she and her two sisters were not to be placed with family after her demise. Some weeks later, my grandmother Maggie Martin-Wright passed away at the age of thirty-two.

When the social worker arrived, my mom obeyed her mother's wishes. As a result, my mother, who was seven years old, the eldest of the three, and her sister Pearl, who was five years old, were placed in a foster home together for a period. In years to come they would be separated for various reasons, one of which was my Aunt Pearls health. Their baby sister, Elaine, who was six to nine months in age was given to her biological father and was never seen again. While in the care of her foster parents, young Dorothy Wright encountered abuse of all kind. This abuse, Mom once confessed, would leave a stain on her heart and mind well into her adulthood.

Despite her very rough beginning, Mom grew into a beautiful woman inside and out. She had the greatest sense of humor and the patience of Job. She was friendly and always had a helping hand for those who were in need. Mom had beautiful bone structure. She would often receive compliments as a young woman, especially when she and my dad were out on the town. Oftentimes when a caregiver came to the home, they would compliment Mom on her skin and her facial features, commenting on how beautiful she was. Mom had high cheekbones that looked as if they had been sculpted and carefully placed on her face. She had the brownest eyes ever and a great smile. She was tall in stature, and in her heyday she was slender and fair in complexion.

Besides being a good-looking woman, Mom was talented, and there was no shortage of her creativity. Mom could sew most anything without a pattern. She would design and manufacture her own drapes, bedspreads, and clothing for herself and our entire family. She would refurbish the furniture all by herself from start to finish. When it came to finances, my mother was very skilled in managing money. No one could save money like my mother; she knew how to squeeze a dollar.

As a young woman, she reconnected with my father, John Walter Weathersby, and they were eventually married. They had known each other since elementary school. Almost daily while they were walking home from school, my dad and his friend, also named John, would tease my mom about how skinny she was. They called her by the name of an old actress, Dorothy Lamour, who was noted for being wafer thin. I once asked my dad why he teased Mom so much when they were children. My dad confessed that it was all love for him, and when he met up with her years later, it was still all love.

During their time together, they managed to raise their children while making great sacrifices along the way. They managed to purchase their own home in Jamaica, Queens, New York. Upon my father's demise after a very short bout with cancer, the family home was sold, and my mother moved to Virginia to be closer to her daughters. Once she arrived in Virginia, she purchased another home outright. True to form, she began making changes to the home—painting and adding a sunroom. A few months prior to his passing, my dad expressed concern about my mother's vision. It was determined that she had glaucoma, which meant that she would experience some loss of vision.

Chapter 2

Change and More Change

Soon after Mom's arrival, we all began noticing that she was having difficulty with her sight, as our father had shared with us earlier, and we also noticed that she was showing signs of mental illness. My older sister was living with Mom during this period. She was supposed to be there to assist Mom in her daily care; it didn't quite work out that way. One day, Mom was left alone. She attempted to cook for herself and left a cloth on the stove. The cloth caught fire. As a result there was extensive damage to the kitchen, but by the grace of God, neither Mom nor her dog was injured. Mom was immediately informed by the fire chief that she would probably not be eligible for fire insurance again. It was in that moment that Mom considered getting rid of her home, and that is exactly what she did.

Mom promptly moved into an independent living community. Shortly after she moved in, Mom began to have hallucinations about various things, but mostly snakes. Not long after she moved in, she was asked to leave, because she continually pulled the emergency alarm when she was hallucinating. Mom's behaviors continued to escalate.

I made an emergency appointment with her doctor. It was my hope that her doctor would prescribe something that would assist in modifying her behavior. Her doctor determined that Mom's heart medication was causing a lack of oxygen to her brain. The lack of oxygen caused her to hallucinate and exhibit strange behaviors, episode after episode. During those times I was called at night to assist with calming her down. There was a final straw, and Mom was asked to leave.

Following her departure from the independent living, Mom moved in with my youngest sister. My sister quickly found it difficult to care for our mother and hold on to a full-time position anywhere. After it was determined that Mom would be moving on, my sister compensated herself financially with Mom's money and sent her to live with my second youngest sister. This would prove to be a poor decision. Mom was constantly neglected; she wasn't fed properly, nor was her medication given to her as it should have been. My sister would often leave our mother in the upstairs bedroom of her town home with little or no light in the room. I would check on her daily, and I would have to feed her, clean up her room, and see to it that she had a bath—all while she lived with my sister. This was heartbreaking and unexpected, considering the fact that Mom went out of her way for my sisters.

There are some things I wish I had done to avoid some of the things I watched my mother go through. I will share with you a couple of important steps to take:

- Recognize the signs—my mother was making poor decisions, because she was experiencing early signs of dementia. Unfortunately, I didn't take the steps necessary to have her evaluated. It would have made it easier to recover what was taken from her at a later day.

- Establish authority—someone has to take the lead, especially when you know that family members are doing things that are unethical and morally wrong. Unfortunately, the events that I described above are more common than they should be. My personal and professional experience is that the first step is to talk to your parent's doctor and ask him to evaluate your parent's mental ability. In order for you to receive power of attorney, your parent must give you authority, or you must establish in a court of law that he or she is unable to attend to his or her own affairs.

8

Chapter 3

It's My Turn Now

When Mom came to live with me after being passed around by all of her children, it happened unexpectedly, and so it goes without saying that I had very little time to prepare. I didn't approve of the things that were transpiring, but I was in the minority in the decision-making process.

One day, Mom showed up at my door with a few items of clothing in her hands. She was wearing clothing that not only didn't match but was not appropriate for the weather. Mom came in and sat down on my couch; she was clearly upset. She stated she hadn't eaten all morning—my sister left her without giving her food or medication again, and she was tired of it. What I was hearing was nothing new. My mother was legally blind, and she struggled mentally in an early stage of dementia. She often braved her way through many obstacles to get to my house for a meal. I witnessed the neglect, but I knew what I would be up against if I made the suggestion that Mom should live with me. But Mom was finally done with the treatment she had been receiving, and she requested to come live with me.

Without even thinking about it, I agreed to let her stay with me. I also contacted my brother and made him aware of our mother's decision. He was not pleased; he had already been poisoned by our sisters. One particular sister was excellent at persuading others and getting them to see things her way. In fact, if by chance it looked as if she was not succeeding in her efforts to sway her target, she would enlist our younger sister to back her up and add credibility to her story. During my conversation with my older brother, he implied that there were concerns with regard to my intentions with our mother's finances. Needless to say, I was livid and hurt, but I was not surprised. To have my motives questioned, especially by those I knew had violated my mother, angered me. My brother was told that I was looking to take my mom's money and live off her. This I found humorous, coming from my sisters. They had some gall, and I made my feelings known.

After many discussions, it was agreed that my brother would kill two birds with one stone. He would come down to retrieve Mom's money from her bank account here in Virginia. He would also visit with mom and other members of the family while he was here. Once he returned to New York, he would establish an account for mom in New York to be used at Mom's request. I agreed to this arrangement it would keep the others from making claims against me while I was caring for our mother, or so I thought. I trusted my brother in spite of his distrust of me; he was financially sound and he had never given me a reason to doubt his honest. I felt it was good to have a system of accountability; someone to verify where her money was going.

Mom moved in that same day. She made it clear that she would only contribute a certain amount to the household monthly. This was fine with me; I worked and had my own income, so it all worked out. It was a few weeks of adjusting furniture, getting rid of items that we no longer had room for, and reassigning sleeping quarters. I moved Mom into one of the girls' rooms. Needless to say, it was a little crowded with the three preteens in one room. It was the perfect formula for daily arguments among the girls.

Mom finally settled in. We kept photos of family members and other items of hers, because we wanted to make it feel like home for her. She appeared to be happy for the moment. There were many adjustments made in the weeks to come, even more than I had anticipated.

Chapter 4

First Things First

Knowing how to consider and address the needs of everyone was the most difficult balancing act I had ever attempted. Integrating an elderly parent with special needs and a few very active pre-teens was difficult enough. Not to mention the unforeseen elements that in some cases, derailed decisions with good intentions—simply didn't work. I also discovered that the caregiver is usually the last to be considered in all of these things, which is the opposite of the way it should be.

This is why it was so important for me to share my family's history with you, the readers. It was pivotal, in that it put into prospective what some of you have already experienced. For others, it will serve as a wake-up call to assist you in deciding how to approach certain aspects of becoming a caregiver of your aging parents.

There has been an upsurge in children caring for ailing parents, which means there is a very good possibility that you or someone you know could be faced with caring for a parent or other loved one. Deciding whether to take the hands-on approach in caring for parents in their twilight years or to place them in the care of others can be very difficult. I have learned that making decisions out of emotion can lead to reparable but long-term issues.

I knew my mother wasn't being cared for properly, and it made the decision that much easier at the time, but I didn't think it through. After all, what was there to think about when I knew for a fact my mother was being neglected? I had to take action. I would never have considered not taking over the care of my mother; however, I would have approached it differently.

Hindsight is twenty-twenty, and looking back, I see it was a major mistake not to consider the other people in my household. I suggest sitting down with your children and other family members and having a real conversation about what it would mean to have an ailing parent in the home. Share the facts with them, and discuss what it may mean to the family as a whole. Give your family members opportunities to express their feelings about the upcoming changes, and validate their concerns. Most of all, try to be truthful and realistic about how you will go about addressing their concerns.

After you have considered everything, should you decide that you don't want to be the hands-on daily caregiver of your parent, there are other alternatives available. Here are just a few:

1. Retirement community—this type of community usually requires that a potential resident be totally independent. Oftentimes they offer dining options, social activities, and minor assistance outside of the realm of personal care. There are some that assist with transportation to events and doctor appointments.

2. Assisted-living community—your parent would have to be somewhat independent. These communities will accept the physically impaired as long as they are mentally functional. There are usually certified nursing assistants (CNAs), personal care assistants (PCAs), and sometimes a registered nurse (RN) on staff in these communities. In most cases, they are there to assist in meal preparations, personal hygiene, and doctor appointments on a short-term basis. Residents must be able to evacuate the premises during an emergency, or they will not be eligible to live there.

3. In-home care—this service requires that your parent or loved one remains either in his or her own home or that of a relative. Service is usually provided by a home health aide, a PCA, or a CNA,

depending on the needs of the patient. All the needs of the client are met in the home. This service is usually limited to a certain number of hours, allotted according to factors such as income, physical needs, and mental ability of the client. Many times a potential client must have a very limited income, with little or no other resources such as saving, stocks and bonds, or property of any kind. If there are any assets that can be liquidated and used for the care of a loved one, the agency, usually the Department of Social Services will require that it be done before they will allow Medicaid to be granted for care. Medicare is oftentimes granted after or around the time of retirement. In our case, it would have been years before my mother would be eligible for any assistance at all through Medicaid. She had owned and sold two homes, and at one point she had CDs and two bank accounts, all of which would have to be exhausted before she could even be considered for help with Medicaid. Mom did have Medicare under my father's social security number after he retired. In the state of Virginia if any property has been sold within the past six months to a year of filing for in-home care assistance, monies generated from that sale must be accounted for and will be considered when it comes to payment of in-home care staff or agencies.

4. Nursing home—this is the least desirable alternative; nursing homes are more often understaffed with bitter, underpaid workers. These individuals have absolutely no incentive to put their best foot forward. I found very few certified nursing assistants who enjoy what they do; as a result many—not all, but many—often administer substandard care to the residents. I cannot tell you the number of times I have heard a certified nursing assistant with whom I have worked say, "I'm not breaking my back for these people; they don't pay me enough for all this." This is a true statement. The average certified nursing assistant earns minimum wage; yet these are the people who care for the disabled, the elderly, and those with long-term illness. I have caught some of the staff yelling, hitting, and even degrading residents or their relatives. Many certified nursing assistants will take revenge on clients for reporting to the administration or even voicing their opinion of the care that they or their loved one is receiving. At a nursing home where my mother was sent for post surgery rehabilitation, a visitor told me that the staff retaliated by feeding

my mother last, because I complained to the director about the care given not only to my mother but also her roommate. They also retaliated by leaving my mother in soiled garments and putting shoes on her that were too small. They had been told several times that the shoes did not belong to her and did not fit. There are a few good nursing homes; however, they are far and few between. You must do your research, including speaking to other residents and their families.

Making the best decision for your parents is difficult, but it is necessary if they are mentally incapacitated. If they are of sound mind, give them their due respect and seek their opinion about how they want to spend the remainder of their time. I have seen people treat their parents with little or no regard, *telling* them what is going to happen instead of including them in the decision-making process.

Taking such liberties can be very demeaning to anyone, let alone your parent. Be wise and kind in the treatment of your parent—I cannot stress this enough. However, in cases where your parent is no longer able to make decisions, don't feel bad about doing so. Hard decisions don't come easily. Check and double-check everything to ensure that your decision will be a sound one.

Chapter 5

Timing Is Everything

Where are you in life? Your station in life is a major factor when considering becoming a full-time caregiver to your parent(s). For example, during this period in my life, I still had children in elementary and junior high school. They were in need of my assistance, and I wasn't always available. In fact, many times my older children had to step in on my behalf. In addition, Mom was not always cooperative, she was incontinent, and sometimes she was combative, depending on who was sitting with her. This made it close to impossible to get anyone to sit with her for any length of time. My children, my mother's granddaughters, stepped in when I really needed someone. I had absolutely no help from any of my siblings at all. My inability to be there for my children during crucial times compromised my relationships with each of them on one level or another.

By the end, they came to resent the fact that it was I—and I alone—who was assuming sole responsibility for my mother's care. It put a lot of strain on the family and the relationships we had. Many of my personal goals were set aside, such as furthering my education, starting a

19

business, and launching out in ministry. I found myself becoming overwhelmed—with no alternatives on most days—I had to weather the storm alone. To add insult to injury, there were virtually no support groups, particularly within the African American community. There were a few organizations that were established by local churches, but not in my community, and when I spoke to them, it appeared they didn't want to venture out of their own communities to assist in another. To my knowledge, there weren't any government-funded organizations at the time, particularly in my area. Also, there were no resources to assist families in connecting to the proper agencies—either for help for the loved one or support for the caregivers. It often came down to whether or not an individual met their criteria, and if the criteria were met, you were faced with tons of paperwork. Fortunately, there have been some improvements in a few of these areas; however, there have not been nearly enough. If you find yourself overwhelmed, or if you are weighing your options, here are a few things you need to know:

- Self-help—Establish your own support team among family and friends if possible. You will need assistance from time to time. As a caregiver, you may find it difficult to even get the time you need to take a relaxing shower or bath. Having time for yourself and your family is critical.

- Assistance from outside sources—if you are faced with looking outside the scope of your family and friends, you must consider community resources. Consider bringing your concerns to your religious leaders. Make the suggestion that they establish an outreach ministry for caretakers. Also, go to your local community centers and inquire about programs they may have available. Make suggestions in support of the caregivers. There are some support groups for caregivers out there, although they are limited in what they can offer in the way of assistance.

- Support groups—establish your own support group. Oftentimes you will come into contact with others who are caring for a parent, at a doctor appointment or senior activities within the community. Reach out to those individuals. It is very likely that they are in the same boat and will benefit from forming and being an active part of a support group.

There are some resources that can assist you in keeping updated on events, availability, and developments in the area of new medications, support services, and changes made to insurance policies and plans, etc.

The following organizations are great resources for caregivers and their loved one for support and useful information.

Agencies

1. CAPS—Children of Aging Parents
2. NCAP—National Caregivers Advisory Panel
3. NFCA—National Family Caregivers Association
4. NCHPP—National Council of Hospice and Palliative Professionals
5. SA—Spouse Association
6. AGIS Network – Assist Guide Information Services
7. AARP—American Association of Retired Persons

On the Internet

1. AgingCare.com
2. Mindingourelders.com
3. ecarediary.com
4. eldercarelocator.com
5. Caregivers Action Network

Chapter 6

The Healthy and Safe Way to Give Care

Once Mom settled in, we were faced with developing her daily routine, which for the most part centered on her doctor appointments. In prior years, Mom had been known for her home treatments. She would always make it a point for all of us to go to the doctor yearly for a major checkup. Everyone in the family was given an examination from head to toe, at which time anything that needed attention was addressed. However, if a health problem arose that could possibly be treated at home; she was going to exhaust all of her remedies before going to the doctor's office.

Mom wouldn't take you to the hospital if you had a lump on your head from a fall, or if you cut your hand open. Mom was the doctor in those cases; she didn't believe in running to the doctor for everything. Many times I felt we should have gone to the doctor, but by the grace of God, it all worked out. When Mom and Dad began to get up in age, the two of them lived at the doctor's office. Over a period of time, the two acquired a host of medications, and that didn't change at all when she came to live with me. Mom had appointment after appointment, constantly having signs of a new ailment. We would check and double-check everything. I took her to the doctor's office so much that, when it was time to make appointment for me or my children, I didn't want to go. I would take my children and forget about myself; sometimes I wouldn't take them unless something was seriously wrong. As a result, when I did go to the doctors after ignoring my health for several years, I was found to have tumors that were the size of a grapefruit, some of which were attached to my intestines. They were so bad that I was given an emergency hysterectomy and, by the grace of God, things went well, and I made a full recovery.

In caring for my mother, I neglected myself and many other areas of importance in my life. There was no balance in any facet of my life. Caring for someone for any length of time requires a lot of mental and physical endurance. When you assume the responsibility of caring for a parent, there is no way of knowing how long you will need to do so. During the twelve years I cared for my mother, I injured my back while attempting to lift her up and out of her wheelchair to put her in bed. I also sustained injuries to my neck, head, legs, and wrist. Many of the injuries I sustained left me with long-term aftereffects. I still experience a great deal of pain in some of the areas where I was injured.

As a caregiver, you are the heart of the family; if the heart fails, everything attached to it dies. You must care for yourself to be effective in caring for others. Because you are providing such extensive care, you must remember to gain knowledge of proper techniques so as not to injure yourself. Using wisdom and resources are essential to providing optimum care safely. Here are just a few things you should know and consider putting into practice while caring for your parent:

- Proper body mechanics—most physical injuries are sustained as a result of using improper body mechanics. If you don't have the skills to provide safe care, you could cause harm to both you and your parent. Learning how to properly transfer your mother or father from a wheelchair to the bed is crucial to prevent back injury. Taking a general course in care giving will help lessen the possibility of injury.

- Proper equipment—there are various companies that sell supports (durable medical equipment) you can wear that will lend support to your body during times of giving personal care such as bathing and lifting your parent. Supports such as back braces, support straps, and wrist bands help to support you. There is also equipment that you can use. The Hoyer lift is a device that assists in lifting and transferring individuals from one area to another. Oftentimes the doctor will prescribe one, in which case it may be covered under an insurance policy.

Chapter 7

There's a Change in the Atmosphere

Over the years, the one thing our home was always noted for was the amount of traffic our family generated. My girls drew the attention of boys and a lot of friends from school. There was no shortage of visitors on the weekends. We enjoyed guests coming over for Bible study, sleepovers, and girls' night, movie night, and theme parties. When Mom became a part of our household, the atmosphere changed a great deal. Because of Mom's dementia, there were moments when having visitors was close to impossible, especially if she believed them to be the enemy. Sudden noises, loud music, and strangers made Mom very uncomfortable. Likewise, the girls, not having a great deal of knowledge of dementia, were less tolerant of Mom's spontaneous behavior. I didn't take the time to explain how dementia affected their grandmother and them. Instead, I would get angry at the fact that they were upset or embarrassed by their grandmother, and I was not empathetic.

I felt like I was constantly defending my right to honor my parents. My father depended on me to care for my mother, and I said I would. I wanted to honor my promise. In the midst of it, my children were affected. I should have validated their feelings and taken a different approach to solving problems.

Overall, the constant changes in her behavior made it difficult to plan anything. Mom's behaviors made the girls ashamed to bring friends around. A house that was once filled with a lot of laughter became a house of contention. They complained constantly about her, and she complained about them. It was awful. After a while, we stopped having friends over as frequently as we had in the past. Our family rarely enjoyed activities in the home together. We didn't go out for girls' night, and the family rarely went out to eat together, attend church services, or go shopping. Someone would have to stay home and keep an eye on Mom. Our time spent together was limited, to say the least, and there was always disruption when Mom was present. It wasn't Mom's fault, and we all understood that; we loved her, and we showed her love all the time. However, even understanding the situation didn't make it easier to do without the things that made us enjoy being a family.

Sometimes I reminisce, and I think of ways we could have included Mom. Things weren't so obvious then; they were a little cloudy. The odd thing is that, looking back from the present time, some of the ways we could have made her a part of things appear so simple. Unfortunately we can't go back, but I will share some of the solutions I have come up with in hopes it will help someone's family:

- Dancing to the music—Mom was unable to see, but it never stopped her from doing the thing she loved the most: dancing. Dancing was something we all enjoyed doing together. Dancing is fun, everyone can do it, and it is great exercise. Find something your loved one wants to do or used to do, and engage them.

- Music appreciation—Opera was a genre of music that my mother enjoyed and appreciated. Her favorite singer was Marion Anderson. Music can be very soothing. It generates a joy that is long lasting and brings forth fond memories. Placing earphones on the ears of your parents to appreciate the music of their era can calm them, and it may afford you the opportunity to watch a movie or play a board game with your family while you all are in the room together. It has been my experience that music is a great tool to use with regard to dementia. The power of music, especially

29

singing, helps unlock memories and stir up the gray areas of memory. It is a very effective means of communication and reaches places in our memory that other treatments can't.

- Reminiscing—Visual prompts are a great way to generate emotion and connect with the past and present. Spend time looking over photos together. Discuss the content. Have your parent try to recall the occasion when the photo was taken. Each time a photo is shown, try to identify the individuals in the photo. Grandparents sharing memories with the grandchildren and other members of the family can be interesting and a lot of fun.

Chapter 8

A Family Divided

Family is extremely important to me, and it had always been my expectation that, in times of trouble, we would all come together. In times past, we always stood together. We saw things through until they were worked out. Imagine the dismay I felt when I came under attack just by virtue of the fact that I chose to honor our mother's request to live with me. Even more disheartening was the motive for all of this animosity I received.

It has been said that money is the root of all evil; this was definitely true in this case. My siblings tried to convince me that it wasn't at all about the money. However, each time we were in a conversation regarding our mother, it was money that led the talks. The concern for our mother's care was never expressed. The questions were always about where and how her money was being used. I suspect it was their inability to access our mother's money at will that really concerned them. Mom's bank account had been all but emptied out; she had about a quarter of what she had when she first arrived in Virginia. My brother, who was in total control of her monies in the bank; sent money only with our mother's consent. I managed her monthly stipend, which wasn't a lot. It covered all of her personal needs, special requests, and contributions to household expenses. Somehow, my family was convinced that I was living high on the hog on our mother's monthly stipend. While I will say that Mom's money helped a great deal after I stopped working outside of the home, it was not my only source of income.

Many people who have not had the experience of caring for a parent or loved one haven't a clue about how much it costs the family—in so many ways. Maintaining employment full time and then coming home and caring for my mother was very difficult—not to mention that I am a mother, and there is no end to that job.

My brother in particular stated that I just wanted to live on Mom's money. He said, "You can work and take care of Mom. You didn't have to stop working. You just don't want to work." I had been working since I was sixteen years old; yet I wanted to stop working for $800 a month. I found that statement laughable, especially coming from the same person who made it a point to tell me that he wouldn't ask his wife to help with his mother. He said, "My wife works, and it would be too much on her to help with Mom."

I thought, *this man is retired and has money. His wife pushes a pencil at work—she is a professor. He never once asked to have his mom come visit for a week. Hiring someone to assist in Mom's care while with him wouldn't have put a dent in his pocket at all.*

My other siblings weren't any kinder, particularly my younger ones. They never supported me in the care of our mother at all, and they spoke ill of me to anyone who would listen. At one point, I told my mother that she was the only reason I had anything to do with any of my siblings. I made it clear that, after her departure, I would probably not have any communication with any of them. Mom expressed her disappointment; she raised us to be close. She felt that, although a lot had transpired, it should not divide us but draw us closer together. She stated that the best thing I could do to honor her after her passing would be to make every effort to keep our family together. I promised her I would try, and I feel that I have, because I believe it is the honorable thing to do.

It is a very unfortunate thing when family begins to turn against one another. I implore you to do everything you can to avoid getting into petty squabbles regarding finances; there is absolutely no good that will come of it. Here are just few steps you should consider to avoid negative feelings generated among family members:

- Make it legal—my parents always told me that if it wasn't in writing, then it didn't exist. If you are the caregiver to your parent, you should have total ability to act on his or her behalf. With permission from your parent, if it is possible, obtain power of attorney. It will legally give you the authority to make decisions for your parent without having to consult with others in the family. That doesn't mean that you should ignore their concerns or not consider their opinion. It just gives you the legal right to make decisions for your parent when it comes to the bottom line. This is a great responsibility in that, should problems arise, you are held totally responsible. Also bear in mind that your power of attorney is only enforceable while the person on whose behalf you are acting is still alive.

- What's in a will—a will is supposed to make things easier; however, you may find that it makes things more difficult. Family members can contest the will. There have been cases where family members challenge the validity of the will just to allow legal fees to deplete the estate of all its financial resources, so no one benefits

34

from the will. Also, when a family member passes away, things do not unfold as you see on television. Unfortunately, there are a few things such as probate court, lawyer fees, and time that come into play.

- Accountability—as a caregiver, you will always be under the microscope of others. Unfortunately, there have been so many caregivers who have taken advantage of their own family members, everyone is suspect. It is wise to have someone who is aware of how the money is being spent. In caring for my mother, I learned that greed will make family members attack you verbally and legally. I have heard of family members taking the caregivers to court both when a parent is still alive and after a parent has passed away. There are family members who will spread lies about you in order to tarnish your reputation and credibility. When family members bring a lawsuit, it often causes a divide that is not easily mended. On the other side of things, if you are the only one providing care, you may feel no obligation to keep anyone informed. If you feel that you might face a legal attack, your best defense is to keep a record of how all monies are spent. If you have to use money from one area to meet a need in another area, do so, but make a note of it. Give an explanation for the move, and explain how you compensated for this move, or if you compensated for it at all. It is better to have your information written down should you have to present your case in court.

- Maintain focus—No matter what you do, keep your focus on your family, and provide the best of care for your parent. You are not obligated to justify your decisions regarding the care and finances of your parent to everyone and anyone who asks. The bigger picture is maintaining harmony among your core family members. Don't allow siblings, cousins, aunts, uncles, and others to come in and cause undue stress for you and your family. When challenged by your family members regarding finances, assure them that everything is being handled properly. Remind them that you have an accountability system in place, and should the time come, you are prepared to answer all questions regarding finances.

After a while, it became obvious that we were in need of a larger place. I decided that moving to a house would be best for all. Mom would have access to a backyard, a porch to get fresh air, and her own room. We would get that extra room that we needed for the girls. Needless to say, we had an increase in our monthly expenses. In fact they skyrocketed, and it was clear additional money was needed. Taking on the additional cost for the larger space—and utilities such as the gas, electric, sanitation, and water—really put a strain on the family. I didn't receive an increase in pay, and Mom's contribution was helpful, but there were a lot of obligations that weren't addressed, because finances were limited. The demands were overwhelming, and despite everything we were going through in the area of finances, there were family members accusing me of taking advantage of Mom. I requested finances for the move and extra bills; I was told that I should find the extra money on my own. I discussed the move and the cost with my mother again, and she authorized the extra monies. It was barely enough, and each month was a struggle.

Chapter 9

Feelings

Providing care to a parent who is mentally and physically incapacitated is very challenging. As time progresses, and your parent's level of functionality decreases, care becomes even more challenging—not just for your parent, but for you, the caregiver. It could also be an emotionally disturbing experience to witness your parent transform into a shell of themselves. Oftentimes my mother would say, "I am a burden to you," or "I should leave, no one wants me here." Those statements couldn't have been further from the truth at first, but those words took on a life of their own. We all began to feel not the burden of her presence, but the burden of trying to keep her reassured and at peace. Finances and feelings overwhelmed me and my immediate and extended family. Not because of my mother, but the lack of planning and the inability to pace myself began making things difficult. If I had the opportunity to do things again I would get to know her better and sooner.

As a child, I always felt somewhat invisible, especially to my parents, unless I got into trouble for some reason. I loved my parents, and for the most part I knew they loved me, although they were not good with verbalizing their feelings. My parents worked hard and provided us with a nice home. Food was plentiful, and there was always someone over for dinner. With all of the friends and family who were present, I felt left out, especially when it came to my mom. She was not the doting mother, in that she wasn't very affectionate. She rarely expressed how she felt about us, unless we did something wrong, and she was angry. As I got older, I didn't have much of a relationship with my mother or my father. The routine was the same every day: we came home from school, changed our clothes, had a snack, completed our homework, and did our chores before we went outside to play. When our parents returned home from work, they would clean up for dinner. At the dinner table, they would discuss everything under the sun that happened throughout the day. It was a time when all matters were addressed, including what we did and didn't do right. So there were not many times when we shared special moments with our father or mother. I suppose there were too many children, too many issues, and not enough hours in the day to give any one child the attention he or she may have desired. Now, having my own children, I understand what a balancing act it was. Even when you think you have done it right, chances are that, in the opinion of your children, you haven't always.

While caring for my mother, I had the opportunity to learn about Dorothy Weathersby, the woman. I knew Dorothy, the mother and the wife, but I never knew her for the woman she was. What I learned about my mother drew me closer to her, and I understood why she was sometimes distant and not affectionate. I learn that my mother's abuse began when she was a child, long before her mother passed away. Mom shared a particular story that brought me to tears. I learn of her aspirations as a young woman to become a nurse; but without the financial support, and having to face the various trials of life, she had to walk away from the idea. She admitted that she regretted not pursuing her goals once things were better.

She shared with me stories of romance, love found and lost, and all of the disappointments and heartaches that came with that. Mom admitted that although the relationship with my dad didn't come without some issues, he was the only man who loved her completely. I enjoyed hearing of her years as an active member of the NAACP when she was a young woman. She spoke of this period fondly and with lots of pride that she'd had a hand in changing a nation.

41

The story that moved me the most and gave me a new outlook on my relationship with Mom was the story of her and my oldest brother, Ronald. Mom was an unwedded teen mom; she was all alone with the exception of her younger sister, Pearl, who stood next to her through it all. Mom told me that her first encounter with my brother was the first time she felt a love that she could not describe. She painted a vivid portrait of holding him in her arms and coming to the knowledge that he was hers—a part of her, someone to love and to love her back—she said my brother made her feel alive for the first time in her life. Needless to say, I cried, and so did she.

I had the opportunity to ask questions about the two of us, and I shared how I felt growing up. She told me that she always loved me, but she had never experienced affection as a child, so she didn't know how to show it. She hugged me and told me she loved me at the conclusion of our conversation—and guess what I did: I cried. This experience left me loving my mother all the more, with a greater understanding of who she was, and our relationship grew.

Don't take your time with your parents for granted. As adults, we often live with things that hurt us as a result of what our parents did or didn't do or say. Take this time to mend the relationships and clear up the issues between you and your parents. Here are just a few things I suggest you do while you still have your parents with you:

- Reconcile—Come to terms with the things that made you unhappy with your parents. There were things about our parents that we didn't like when we were children; they made you feel badly about how they treated you, communicated with you, or disciplined you. Talk to your parents about those issues before they are gone forever. You might discover some things that will change your outlook on your relationship with your parents. Overall, the word is *forgiveness*. Forgive them no matter what, for their peace and yours.

- Show them love before it's too late—the latter days of your parents' life are so important. It is your opportunity to bring peace and joy to life that will allow them to move on into eternity without fears or regret. Showing them lots of physical love, even if that was never the nature of your relationship, will help bring comfort and leave a lasting impression on your memory that will help you through the rough patches. I can tell you from experience that those days of showing my mother love are the ones that bring me joy when she comes to my memory.

Chapter 10

Just Before He Called

The day my mother went to be with our Father, I woke up that morning feeling afraid and filled with anxiety. She had been hospitalized after having surgery on her gall bladder. It was supposed to be a simple operation. Afterward, there were a few complications; one of the complications was the fact that my mom could not walk at all. She couldn't even stand. At first, I thought it was due to the anesthesia; however, the doctor said it was the combination of her age and going through surgery.

The second problem that arose after surgery was that Mom contracted a common infection known as Clostridium difficile, also known as C. diff. I was told by the doctor that this was a common occurrence; she would recover after a few days of receiving treatment. Although Mom recovered from the C. diff, she was still in need of rehabilitation, because she was unable to walk. The doctor stated that this was also a common occurrence with elderly patients.

The doctor sent my mom to a local nursing home to be rehabilitated. That was a nightmare. The nurses and aides were overworked and underpaid, and it showed in their work performance and attitudes. The nursing home reeked of urine and feces, and we could always find the nurses and their aides in a room located near or behind the desk, hiding from their duties.

Mom's condition worsened due to the very poor care that she was given by the health-care professionals there. Mom was rushed to the hospital after I found her one day, slumped over in her chair with the door to her room closed. Her shirt was covered in vomit, and her clothing was soaked with urine and excrement. Needless to say, I was livid, and I demanded that my mother be removed from the facility at once. Although I repeatedly requested an explanation in writing as to why my mother was in that condition, I never received one.

Once she was in the hospital, it was determined that Mom's condition had progressed to Alzheimer's, and she would probably not recover. Ultimately, the doctor gave Mom a few weeks to live. She was receiving oxygen and being treated for the intestinal infection. I didn't want to believe the doctor's report, and so I prayed that God would prolong my mother's life.

After praying for a week for Mom's recovery, one morning I received a peace about Mom's condition and her going home. God is so awesome that he put it in my heart to ask her how she felt about how she lived her life. To my amazement Mom, in her weakened state, said in a very strong and confident tone, "I've lived a good life, I have been blessed beyond measure, a life I never expected to have; God has given me more than enough." A joy and peace rose up inside of me. I asked the doctor if he was going to let her go home, and he said yes. Mom was put in the hospice program, she was given everything needed to keep her comfortable at home.

The weeks that followed were extremely difficult at times; Mom's condition continued to worsen. At one point she stopped eating, and her hands looked blue. With every change I called the doctor or the hospice nurse, and they would walk me through the steps.

I called everyone to tell them that Mom had but hours to live, according to hospice. My sister came over. She walked into Mom's room; she wasn't in the room long before she began calling me. I instantly knew why she was calling me. When I reached the side of her bed, we both were in a haze, so we called my sister's boyfriend into the room, and he confirmed that Mom was gone. It was like an out-of-body experience—unbelievable.

No summary, commentary, or suggestion can brace you for this moment.

Chapter 11

It's All Over Now

The next morning was a blur. There I was, feeling drained and somewhat lost; I had a lot ahead of me. Planning a funeral is never easy; however, it is even more difficult when it's for your parent. And not just a parent, but one to whom you devoted twelve years of your life. The first thing I did after I woke was go to my mother's bedroom. Part of me was still in a state of shock; I found it difficult to believe that my mother was no longer here with me. I hesitated and then pushed the door open. The room had a looming presence, one that I couldn't identify. The empty bed and the vision of the undertaker removing my mother's body sent the pain of her loss rushing back in. Soon after, I felt relief, which led to my feeling guilty for feeling relieved. I was, for certain, on an emotional roller coaster.

The passing of my mother left as many questions as there were emotional changes, if not more. It signified the end of one era and the beginning of another, with the latter era filled with uncertainty. As a caregiver, my time had been consumed with caring for the needs of my mother, my children, and many others, all of this while making every attempt to maintain my household and financial stability. During this twelve-year journey I made many sacrifices on every level, but in doing so, I acquired some very important information that will surely be beneficial to individuals who are considering caring for a parent or other loved one. As I reflect on my role as a caregiver, a daughter, a mother, and a woman—along with many other hats I have worn—I am most certain that if it were not for the Lord Jesus Christ, my Savior; my God, who is the head of my life; and the Holy Spirit, my guide to all truth, teaching, and comfort, I could not have survived. I would not have come through all that I faced in caring for my mother if it were not for God's grace and mercy.

I know that there are many who have faced and are now facing caring for a parent. Until you have actually done so, you will never know the full magnitude of what it entails. I worked in the field as a CNA for years, and it did not prepare me for what I experienced. I thought my experience as a CNA would give me an edge in caring for my parent, but I was blindsided. There were so many things I missed, yet nothing took away from the privilege of caring for the most important woman in my life: my mother, Dorothy Weathersby.

Giving great care is one of the biggest contributions one can make, and I am convinced that sharing my experience with others will help them avoid the pitfalls and make sound decisions. It is my prayer that each reader will take something away, something that will be of some assistance in caring for their loved one.